OVERCOMING SUICIDE

How to overcome suicide and live a victorious Life

Ruth Jackson

<u>Dedication</u>

To God, the father; for preserving my life from the hades of death, for eternal life through the salvation of Jesus Christ

And

To my parents; my father, The Rev. Dr. Jackson, for being the most wonderful dad in the world, for inspiring me to be the best that I can. To my mother, Margaret, for being the best mother. You brought me up with all the love there is, and you still do. I love you.

Contents

<u>Acknowledgements</u>

My two sons, Jackson and Paul;you are the apple of God's eye. I am honored to be the one you call mom.

My husband George, what can I say? Thank you for loving me and making me smile on most days, for your relentless support.

My lecturers, Prof. Micheal Ayeli and Dr. Samuel Kamau; thank you for your follow-up, to making sure my piece is excellent.

My brothers Tim and Isaac, your support and love is unmatched, I could never ask for more.

My mother in love Nelas; you are one of a kind.

CHAPTER 1

<u>My Story</u>

It was the last Sunday of my life, and I had everything planned out in my head. I had made the decision to end my life, and that was the end of it. I'd be alone at home that afternoon and take poison, which would work because no one would be there to save me.

I grew up in church because my parents are devout pastors who took us to church since we were infants. Church was and continues to be an important part of my life. As it was the last Sunday of my life, I reasoned, it was critical that I attend church as a hobby. I went to our Christian union at the university as usual, and then to this new church that I had discovered. I had come to admire how the church's Bishop, taught the Word of God.

I waited patiently for the bishop to take the stage and preach so that I could go home and take my life, finally leaving this world behind. The moment arrived, but to my dismay, he was not present, and an associate pastor was in charge.

My initial instinct was to leave, but I was seated right at the front and lacked the nerve to stand up in front of everyone who was staring at me because I had only just came in, not to mention my large suitcase. Despite the fact that it was many years ago, the sermon he gave on fatherhood has never left my memory. I just sat there waiting for him to finish so that I could go and "rest,"

He finished at last! He remained still as he observed the gathered people. I'll never forget what he said. "There are seven persons in this room who are suicidal in spirit. Actually, some of you are prepared for today. The Holy Spirit is asking me to tell you to come to the front so that I can pray for you." I froze. My entire body was dumb. I wouldn't move. I felt somebody was interrupting my plans and I didn't like it. A few people stepped up, but I declined. He wasn't rushing, either. "There are yet more, we're ready and waiting for you." He insisted.

As much as I was thinking of suicide, I was still born again and a devoted member of the worship team at the University. I was having a walk with God, but I was bitter and frustrated with life for absolutely no reason, I mean! I had everything I needed at this time in my life. I was pursuing my dream course, in my dream university. I had my parents and siblings who loved me terribly and I knew it. I had everything I could possibly need. There was nothing that I could attribute to being dismal and making me consider suicide. I just felt awful and useless in this world, without a reason to even exist.

I sat there, debating with God and telling him I was tired of living and he should just leave me alone, but within a short while, I found myself at the altar. Praise be unto Jesus! Looking back, I know God purposefully placed me close to the altar because I would never have had the confidence to approach it entirely from behind.

I sobbed at the altar because of the presence of the Holy Spirit's might. I could close my eyes and still hear the pastor's words. "These folks have a great destiny. The enemy seeks to destroy them because they have a purpose in life."

If you are contemplating suicide and you are reading this, I have to tell you that you are the best thing that could have ever occurred. You are an amazing person. Your destiny and mission on this planet are unique. The enemy knows this and wants to destroy you because of it. But right now I take power and authority in the name of Jesus and I pray that yoke of suicide is broken.

I met with Jesus at the altar. He was present in all his love and tranquility. The preacher broke the shackles of suicide by praying for us. I was a different person than the one who had just woken up from it as I made my way back to my seat. An encounter with Jesus even just for a minute is a life changing event. Don't go too far, if you desire that encounter, you can have it anywhere, even alone in your bedroom, and I will be telling you about it in my next chapters. I felt peace. I felt loved, a kind of love I can't explain. I experienced a tremendous weight being lifted off of me. I once again had the need to live. Suicidal thoughts stopped immediately and for good. Hallelujah! Since that time, many years have gone, and although I have experienced many dramatic storms, I have never considered suicide. Simply because suicide is a spirit of death from hell and all you need is to rebuke and tell it off

<u>Uncle P's Story</u>

It was over the Christmas holiday. I had just finished my final high school exam and was looking forward to a Christmas without school! My high school was more like a military camp than a school, and surviving four years was cause for celebration. That was going to be the best Christmas in a long time, or so I thought!

We were watching my favorite soap opera after dinner when my father received a phone call. He quickly excused himself and entered their bedroom. In a fraction of a second, his expression had changed. He was drenched in shock. I was intrigued. I couldn't hear the other person, but his response bothered me. I followed him and stood at the door, listening in. Someone had died, and it was someone close to us. I'd tell it in my father's voice. He was devastated and taken aback. 'From where did it happen, at home or in the hospital?" I recall his perplexed voice asking. The call went dead, and silence descended. I dashed back to the sitting room so he couldn't catch me at the door. I was terrified. My conscience warned me that something was seriously wrong.

Dad took a long time to return to the sitting room, and when he did, his face was washed with sadness. He'd been crying, which we didn't see very often. He uttered not a single word. He simply sat there. He just sat there, staring blankly at the TV. I waited for him to say something, but he didn't.

I stayed awake for most of the night, wondering who had died. According to my father's response, it was one of the people who lived at my mother's ancestral home. Against all odds, I hoped it wasn't uncle P, who was one of them. I hoped it was someone far away, someone I didn't recognize. Uncle P had a special place in my heart.

We had run into him in the nearby town two weeks before, along with my mother; his sister. His wife, three-year-old son, and three-month-old daughter accompanied him. We ordered tea and *mandazi*. I was overjoyed to see them all. I argued with him about not sending me a success card during my final exams, which I had been waiting for; it was the rage back then. He promised to send me a Christmas card that year, and I naturally believed him. We said our goodbyes. When you were a minor, back then, you were not entitled to your own mobile phone, so you spoke to people in your inner circle when you met them, or you wrote a letter that took weeks to be delivered and returned. As a result, that meeting was significant for me, and I have kept it in my memory.

My father left early the following morning before we were awake. My mother was away for her summer semester in the University and they were about to break for Christmas.

When Dad returned home that evening, his normally light complexion had darkened significantly. It was postmortem day, and he had gone along with the rest of the brothers. He was depressed, very depressed.

He broke the news and confirmed my worst fear; uncle P was dead. My heart was broken. I was devastated, I couldn't cry out the pain. That was a pain that took years to heal!

I locked my gaze on him as he lay silently in the coffin. It had been a nightmare. My body's strength had vanished. From behind, a strong hand gripped me tightly. I had been warned not to view the body, but I was in denial and that was the only way I could accept it. It took a long time to recover from that loss and pain.

<u>Brian's Story</u>

On my way home, I stood at the stage, waiting for the bus. I had just returned from a sleepover with my girlfriend. The sound of the engine caused me to turn around and stare at the fast-moving vehicle. It was a classic-looking race car. "This is a simple but very classic car, the graphics and the sound of the engine," I remember thinking to myself. The car pulled up next to me and stopped, much to my surprise. The driver waved as he rolled down his window. I thought he'd read my mind, but it turned out to be a very good friend of mine, Brian! (not his real name). I hopped into car.

Brian was my desk mate best friend in primary school. However, we had lost contact after primary school, but here we were, after all these years. We had a lot of ground to make up.

We dropped something off at his house on our way to town for a cup of coffee. I was surprised at how quickly he had advanced. He graduated a year before I did. He was already married with a son and living in his mansion with an upstairs. I admired him. I had a stressful job and a failing relationship. I'd rented a one-bedroom apartment and was scraping by. I was delighted for him. He had made significant progress in a short period of time. He'd turned into a racer. He was brimming with energy, happiness, friends, and, of course, money.

We raced along the superhighway as the *matatus* gave us the right of way, which they never do in our city. Several passengers peered out the window. We were the stars of the show. "You seem so at ease; have you ever been in a race car?" He inquired. "No, but I enjoy speed!" I replied. It was a lot of fun! We were young and didn't have much to lose. We exchanged phone numbers as he drove me home. I did, however, say a prayer for him. I begged the Lord not to let him die in an accident. I wish I had simply prayed to the Lord to preserve his life, but how was I supposed to know?

After a while, Brian found everyone we went to primary school with and formed a WhatsApp group. I'll never understand how he did it. Our primary school years were filled with wonderful memories. Everyone was someone's brother or sister. The teachers adored us because we were the first class to achieve the highest mini-score. It was a joyful reunion. Brian was the type of person who knew everyone and was always available when you needed him.

I was preparing dinner when my phone received a WhatsApp message . It was from one of my former classmates. 'Brian, our brother, died at his home…" I did not finish the message. I yelled. We had spoken with Brian the week before. He was fine and in good health. At the time, my husband came and stayed with me. I dialed his best friend's number. My intention for calling was for him to inform me that Brian was not dead, but he did worse. He was in a worse condition than I was. To say the least, he was enraged, hurt, and devastated. Brian had hung himself using cloth lines at his house around 1.20 a.m. the night before. He'd been curious enough to tilt the cc camera and record himself to save his family the trouble of investigation. Brian had not left a note. He just left the house after a long angry conversation on phone, as the cc camera revealed, and rushed to the hanging lines.

I stared at Brian, neatly shaven, lying in his coffin. He was dressed in one of his favorite outfits, a white t-shirt and white jeans. He was so young, only 33 years old. I couldn't believe he was gone. My heart was breaking for his children and their mothers. His son was nine years old, his daughter was younger, and another child was on the way. My heart ached for his parents and siblings. He was their last child. That was a sad day that was followed by many more days, months, and years of pain and grief.

CHAPTER 2

THE REAL CAUSE OF SUICIDE

Uncle P woke up from his coffin and said hi to me. We were many but he just chose me. I woke up from the dream with a deep sense of loss and grief. Just a few minutes we were with him, or so I felt and saw in my dream. He was so real and a sense of fulfillment washed me away in that dream, and waking up to the reality that he was dead gave me so much pain.

I experienced several dreams of the kind during that period. I looked forward to sleep so that I could 'meet' him. I tell you what that was the same period I was suicidal! As I explained to you earlier, I had nothing physical disturbing me at the time I was suicidal, but during the time, the spirit of suicide would visit me in my dreams and cause me to be miserable and just wish for death.

There is only was cause of suicide and that's the spirit of death, made in the pit of hell by Lucifer himself. You or your loved one may have a physical reason for suicide such as financial stress, relationship stress and many more reasons that lead people to being depressed and finally taking their lives. All these reasons are simple tactics from the enemy to take your life or your loved one.

John 10:10

The enemy came to kill, steal, and destroy, but I have come that you may have life and life indeed.

The sole reason that the enemy came, was to kill; suicide is one of his most powerful tactics.

The Doorways Of Suicide

Sin

Matthew 27: 3

Then Judas, His betrayer, seeing that He had been condemned, was remorseful and brought back the thirty pieces of silver to the chief priests and elders, 4. saying, "I have sinned by betraying innocent blood." And they said, "What is that to us! See unto it! 5. Then he threw down the pieces of silver in the temple and departed, and went and hanged himself.

One of the attributes of God is holiness. We are the temple of the Holy spirit.

1 Corinthians 6 19

Or do you not know that your body is the temple of the Holy Spirit *who is* in you, whom you have from God, and you are not your own?

God cannot live in an unholy temple. The emptiness in your soul caused by the absence of the Holy Spirit because of sin opens the door for the enemy to control your life. Again, his only mandate is to kill, destroy and steal. Look at the case of Judas Iscariot. The enemy used him to betray Jesus, and eventually killed him through suicide because of that sin.

Brethren, are you living in sin? The enemy is not your friend. He is a deceiver and all he will do is destroy your life:

The wages of sin is death

Romans 6:23

23 For the wages of sin is death, but the free gift of God is eternal life through Christ Jesus our Lord.

Disobeying the voice of God either in your secret place with him or in his word is also a grave mistake that would buy you a ticket to trouble causing you to take your life away.

1 Samuel 15:22-23

"Has the LORD as great delight in burnt offerings and sacrifices, as in obeying the voice of the LORD? Behold, to obey is better than sacrifice, and to listen than the fat of rams. For rebellion is as the sin of divination, and presumption is as iniquity and idolatry. Because you have rejected the word of the LORD, he has also rejected you from being king."

Be careful to obey the instructions given to you by the holy spirit through his still small voice or in his word. Sometimes, and most times, God doesn't make sense in his instructions, but later on you realize he was right all the way

Isaiah 55:8-9

8 "For my thoughts are not your thoughts,

  neither are your ways my ways,"

declares the LORD.

9 "As the heavens are higher than the earth,

  so are my ways higher than your ways

  and my thoughts than your thoughts.

<u>Generational curses</u>

During the period that I was suicidal in my case, the same spirit of suicide that had taken uncle P, was the one visiting me in my dreams. I was a second generation from him in the family. Have you had of a family that people die of a certain cause; either suicide, accidents or certain chronic diseases?

I must take this opportunity to let you note that dreams with the dead whether due to suicide or not are evil plans from hell to kill you. The faces you see in the dreams are not the real people but demons carrying the spirit of death. It is hence your role to wake up and rebuke the spirit of death in the name of Jesus as you have been given power and authority to rebuke the enemy.

John Ramirez, a former Satanist disclosed in one of his books that they would visit the burial of a person and at the graveside since the family members were present, they would search for a person whom they would throw at the spirit from hell that tormented the deceased in his lifetime. Evil spirits are generational. They seek to dominate a family from generation to the other.

Deuteronomy 5:9

For I, the Lord your God, *am* a jealous God, visiting the iniquity of the fathers upon the children to the third and fourth *generations* of those who hate me.

The enemy uses this principal in the bible as a doorway and legal right to visit families. That is why you may observe that some families struggle with a certain oppression such as poverty, certain illness, early death, drunkenness, polygamy or sexual immorality and many more.

We later found out that Brian's grandfather, the one he had been named after had committed suicide at a young age. Looking at Brian, he had everything going well for him, money and family. He was steps ahead from his peers. But the same spirit that took his grandfather came for him. Unfortunately he didn't have someone to pray and break that stronghold in his life.

The good news is that we have been given power and authority to break strongholds that rule in our families. Praying, invoking the blood of Jesus and his word, fasting, and laying a sacrifice at the altar are tools to break evil altars dominating in a family. It is also crucial to visit a higher authority that you are sure about to pray for you.

Depression

Depression is the leading the cause of suicide in the world in layman's what language. This is the aftermath of the enemy attacking your life let's say through broken families broken love, poverty, loss of finances, rejection, and whatever else that may have caused depression in you or your loved one. I have good news for you though. Did you know that you can have joy, peace, love, during a very trying moment?

I experienced a very tough financial season of my life. At one point, I grew into depression. I was worried because my two boys were under the age of three whom I loved and were depending on me as their mother. I realized I hated taking a bath. A week and sometimes even two would pass by without one. I am thankful to my understanding husband who never pressurized me at this time because of my look. I had completely let go off myself. I would wake up with a horrible mood for no reason at all. I felt miserable and horrible about my life. You will be surprised at this season, I was not suicidal and this was simply because as I had explained, the spirit of suicide in my life had been rebuked by a man of God years ago and that was the end of its stronghold in my life.

However, the fact that I was jobless had started to take a toll in me. I knew if I lost myself my kids would suffer, the last thing I wanted as a mother. Well, my financial status did not change then, but in the middle of it, I found joy and peace and slowly depression in my life vanished out of the window. In fact, I remember one day my mother was on a video call with us and the kids and was surprised of the joy and happiness that was in my house despite the financial strain.

Come with me; let's study this verse and what Jesus says about being emotionally burdened. The word of God is life and true. God has exalted himself above his word and he watches over to accomplish it. His word is true and he cannot lie, nor forget, nor change his mind. Whatever he says, that's what he does, all you have to do is believe.

Isaiah 61:1-3

61 "The Spirit of the Lord God is upon Me,

Because the Lord has anointed Me

To preach good tidings to the poor;

He has sent Me to [a]heal the brokenhearted,

To proclaim liberty to the captives,

And the opening of the prison to those who are bound;

2 To proclaim the acceptable year of the Lord,

And the day of vengeance of our God;

To comfort all who mourn,

3 To [b]console those who mourn in Zion,

To give them beauty for ashes,

The oil of joy for mourning,

The garment of praise for the spirit of heaviness;

That they may be called trees of righteousness,

The planting of the Lord, that He may be glorified.”

Look at verse 3. That heaviness you are feeling is a spirit and Jesus says he wants to lift it up and give you a spirit of praise. Selah! It doesn't matter the reason for the heaviness. I am not trying to dispute the fact that what you are going through is not a weighty matter. It is, but guess what? Jesus knows about that, and he has come to lift it out and replace the spirit of heaviness with the garment of praise! All you have to do is ask him every morning.

During this season of my life, this word was my bread. I woke up every day and asked the lord to lift away the heaviness I felt in my spirit and give me a spirit of praise. Are you in mourning? Have you lost something? Probably a relationship, a marriage, money, has your spouse left for another person and the pain and grief is taking a toil in your spirit? Guess what, the lord understands the pain, and the mourning and he came to lift it up and instead give you the oil of gladness. Oh that oil! Nothing, no one can give it to you! I realized every day I would pray with this verse, I was happy and joyful. The Holy Spirit would open up my eyes to see so many more blessings in my life that money would not buy.

With time, depression vanished in my life. I did not go for counseling nor, seek medication. I am not disputing the power of counseling and medication. If the depression is at an advanced stage, this is highly recommended. You can combine the 3, prayer, medication and counseling. In my case, I would not afford medication nor counseling as I was financially crippled. I was not also willing to put the burden on my parents or family. I was also afraid of the stigma, incase other people came to learn about it! Isn't great how God heals you and never stigmatizes you, nor announces your problems to the whole world?

Your joy, peace of mind is found in Christ Jesus alone and not earthly possessions or people.

CHAPTER 3

LIFE AFTER SUICIDE

There is no eternal peace after suicide; only much more agony in hell!

It is sad that people commit suicide thinking they're going to have eternal peace and rest forever, only to realize they were wrong after it is too late. If you are reading this book and have suicidal thoughts, please, please, come with me and let's study what the word of God says about that. Then you can make your choice. Please do not take your life away because where you will be landing next is a million times worse to whatever you are going through at this moment. If your loved one is in the verge of suicide, please make her or him aware of the knowledge of God as well.

You were created in the image of God and his breath. It is easy to assume that after death, the way the body seems to appear in the morgue, eyes closed, no moving, no hearing, no singing, and you think that the person have rested; it is a big lie!

Genesis 2:7.

And the Lord God formed man *of* the dust of the ground, and breathed into his nostrils the breath of life; and man became a living being.

God created your body using dust in his likeness. That is what dies and goes back to dust. He also breathed his life in you so that you became a living thing, so guess what? you carry the very breath of God which never dies and that is your soul.

During the first death of the body the soul returns to its maker and depending on if you had the covenant of salvation with Jesus Christ, you go hell or heaven.

Mathew 13:42

And will throw them into the furnace of fire; in that place there will be weeping and gnashing of teeth.

Matthew 25:41

"Then He will also say to those on His left, 'Depart from Me, accursed ones, into the eternal fire which has been prepared for the devil and his angels

Exodus 20:14. "You shall not murder.

According to the word of God, murdering yourself is a crime. You do not belong to yourself, but unto God. The life you carry is his life which you should not kill!

1 Corinthians 6:9

Do you not know that the unrighteous will not inherit the kingdom of God? Do not be deceived.

When you die in sin, you cannot simply inherit his kingdom, which is a straight ticket to hell.

2 Thessalonians 1:8.

Taking vengeance on those who do not know God, and on those who do not obey the gospel of our Lord Jesus Christ. 9. These shall be punished with

everlasting destruction from the presence of the Lord and from the glory of His power,

My brother my sister, suicide is breaking the law of our Lord Jesus Christ; do not kill. As such, the punishment is everlasting destruction in hell.

Matthew 13:42

And will throw them into the furnace of fire; in that place there will be weeping and gnashing of teeth.

Matthew 25:41

"then he will also say to those on his left, 'depart from me, accursed ones, into the eternal fire which has been prepared for the devil and his angels

Matthew 10:28

Do not fear those who kill the body but are unable to kill the soul; but rather fear him who is able to destroy both soul and body in hell.

Mark 9:43-48

"if your hand causes you to stumble, cut it off; it is better for you to enter life crippled, than, having your two hands, to go into hell, into the unquenchable

fire, [where their worm does not die, and the fire is not quenched.] "if your foot causes you to stumble, cut it off; it is better for you to enter life lame, than, having your two feet, to be cast into hell,

What is this so important, more than your life, that you want to throw yourself in the hades of fire and worms for eternity? Who is this so big and important that you want to throw yourself into the eternal fire, because he or she left or hurt you? You carry all your senses in hell or in heaven; pain, happiness, hopelessness, fear, etc. If you are planning to take your life away, please, please, please, remember you will be sending yourself into much more agony and pain that you can never imagine.

The person who hurt you is not worth throwing yourself into eternal fire and anguish. The thing you have lacked probably education, money or some of that thing you think you need are not worth you throwing yourself to eternal flames.

If guilt won't let you go like Judas Iscariot, there is forgiveness of your soul as I will further explain to you in the next chapters.

Mark 8:36.

For what will it profit a man if he gains the whole world, and loses his own soul?

You would rather miss out on that very thing that makes you feel you cannot live without and live to go to heaven where there is joy and happiness.

The Damage Left On Your Loved Ones After Suicide

It took me years before healing uncle P's death. I felt guilty for not telling him how much he meant to me , the last day we had bumped with him in town. I wished over and over again that I would have been at his home the day he hang himself. I can only imagine what his young wife went through after that. His kids, who are my cousins are still coming to terms with that loss to date. Writing about this hurts me deeply and I wish to put a comma about the present in that matter. Do you want to live behind the people whom you love and love you in a forever misery? Think about it.

Brain's first son was 9 when he died. I can still recall the sadness in him as he slowly carried the cross to the grave side. That sight is still fresh in my memory. "Didn't Brian think of his kids first before killing himself?" I remember one of our friends asking as we drove out of the morgue to his home.

Death is the saddest affair on earth. It leaves wounds that only God can heal and give you strength and peace to cope with. In real sense, those scars never heal, and when visited, they never stop to ache. I wish you could spare your loved ones from such pain.

<u>Healing From The Loss Of A Person Who Committed Suicide</u>

We all heal differently and healing comes in stages. It is just like a physical wound that heals with time but leaves a big scar.

Denial

The first stage of grief is denial. You imagine you are dreaming and everyone else is making a mistake on the identity of the person. Sometimes the first thing you do is dial the deceased's number and expect him or her to pick up or return your call as always. Medically, this is a self defense method to prevent you from getting into shock. Attending the burial of the person either online if you cannot make it or physically helps in having closure. Viewing the body also brings closure, but this is a personal choice. In the event you are not strong enough or have no desire to, you do not have to view the body.

Anger

It is normal for one to be bitter with both God and the deceased, or one of them. Sometimes you feel like you would give them a thorough beating for causing you so much pain. At this stage, some people will easily throw things at the wall and wail loudly. It is okay. Allow yourself to let out the pain instead of enclosing it inside. I must note that it is wrong to tell a mourning person to stop crying and to be strong. Instead of helping that person, you are throwing them in a sea of more pain as you are stopping them from letting out their pain from within. It is recommendable to give a shoulder to a mourning person and let them cry, until they cannot cry anymore. You do not have to say anything. Just being there is enough for them sometimes.

Bargaining

At this stage, guilt is common. You tend to imagine that you would have prevented the person from suicide. You would have them loved them differently. You would have told them about Christ. You need to forgive yourself and understand there is nothing you would have done to help the person because you did not know that he or she would end his or her life. Again, the sole decision to take his or her life was entirely on him/her and not you. Whether you are to blame as the suicidal note read or not, the decision to take the life was entirely on the deceased and not you.

Again, if you contributed to the thoughts of suicide, you must forgive yourself and allow yourself to heal. Self forgiveness is the beginning of healing from the guilt. You must also forgive the deceased for eventually taking his or her life and leaving you in the sea of pain. At this point, nothing we can do to bring back the life, only learn to live with the loss. As harsh as it is, but it is the reality.

Depression

At this stage, the bargaining is no longer there. You realize the person is never coming back even after all the bargaining and there is nothing you can do to change the situation. This stage comes with a deep sense of loneliness and feeling absence the person. Sometimes you may see something that completely resembles something of the deceased or even someone, only to understand that's not it.

Acceptance

After depression, the reality of the absence of the person slowly starts to be accepted. You may remember the beautiful memories made and start to celebrate. It is in most cases an upward turn of events. You start having hope and life around you. You are also aware of other good things around you that bring life to you. It is usually the last stage of grief.

Grief is the hardest thing to deal with because there is nothing you can do to escape it. However, in this period of time, hold on to **Isiah 61:3 to give them the oil of gladness instead of the spirit of mourning , and the garment of praise instead of the spirit of heaviness**. Pray with this word every day or every hour when you feel that the pain is unbearable.

He binds up the broken hearted.

Psalm 147:3

New King James Version

3 He heals the brokenhearted and binds up their wounds.

CHAPTER 4

HOW TO OVERCOME THE SPIRIT OF SUICIDE

Praise And Worship

Praise is the art of lifting and clapping your hands and probably shouting about the goodness of God. What he has done for you and all his wonderful works on earth. You can tell him or tell about him. It could be in song or word of mouth or screams and shouts.

Worship is the art of talking to God directly to him and adoring him of whom he is. Worship has nothing to do with what you are going through but all the attributes of God. His holiness, greatness, faithfulness etc.

Let's have a tour at the throne of heaven where worship happens for eternity.

Revelation 4:8

The four living creatures, each having six wings, were full of eyes around and within. And they do not rest day or night, saying: "Holy, holy, holy, Lord God Almighty, Who was and is and is to come!" 9. Whenever the living creatures give glory and honor and thanks to Him who sits on the throne, who lives forever and ever, 10. The twenty-four elders fall down before Him who sits on the throne and worship Him who lives forever and ever, and cast their crowns before the throne, saying: 11. "You are worthy, O Lord, To receive glory and honor and power; For You created all things, And by Your will they exist and were created."

Revelation 5:11

Then I looked, and I heard the voice of many angels around the throne, the living creatures, and the elders; and the number of them was ten thousand times ten thousand, and thousands of thousands, 12. Saying with a loud voice: "Worthy is the Lamb who was slain To receive power and riches and wisdom, And strength and honor and glory and blessing!" 13. And every creature which is in heaven and on the earth and under the earth and such as are in the sea, and all that are in them, I heard saying: "Blessing and honor and glory and power Be to Him who sits on the throne, And to the Lamb, forever and ever!" 14. Then the four living creatures said, "Amen!" And the twenty-four elders fell down and worshiped Him who lives forever and ever.

These are my favorite verses. Every time I worship the Lord joining the 24 elders and angels numbering thousands and ten thousands and the four living creatures and all creatures in heaven and on the earth and in the sea and all that is in it, the sweet presence of the Lord just invades me. There is nothing as wonderful as the very sweet presence of God.

Psalms 16:11

You will show me the path of life; In Your presence is fullness of joy; At Your right hand are pleasures forevermore.

You can worship God right inside your bedroom, inside your car, or wherever you are. You do not have to wait for Sunday during the praise and worship session.

Praise and worship brings down the presence of God to where you are.

Psalms 22: 3. But you are holy and inhabits the praises of Israel, your people.

The mere presence of the Lord caused Jordan to pull back. When Israel praised him (Judah means praise) he inhabited their praise and let's see what happened.

Psalm 114

When Israel went out of Egypt,

The house of Jacob from a people of a strange language,

2 Judah became His sanctuary,

And Israel His dominion.

3 The sea saw it and fled;

Jordan turned back.

4 The mountains skipped like rams,

The little hills like lambs.

5 What ails you, O sea, that you fled?

O Jordan, that you turned back?

6 O mountains, that you skipped like rams?

O little hills, like lambs?

7 Tremble, O earth, at the presence of the Lord,

At the presence of the God of Jacob,

8 Who turned the rock into a pool of water, The flint into a fountain of waters.

The presence of the Lord also causes demons to bow down, before he even speaks. Lets look at what happened to the man who was possessed with many demons and nobody would bind him because the demons were too strong.

Mark 5:1

Then they came to the other side of the sea, to the country of the Gadarenes. 2. And when He had come out of the boat, immediately there met Him out of the tombs a man with an unclean spirit, 3. Who had his dwelling among the tombs; and no one could bind him, not even with chains, 4. Because he had often been bound with shackles and chains. And the chains had been pulled apart by him, and the shackles broken in pieces; neither could anyone tame him. 5. And always, night and day, he was in the mountains and in the tombs, crying out and cutting himself with stones. 6. When he saw Jesus from afar, he ran and worshiped Him. 7. And he cried out with a loud voice and said, "What have I to do with You, Jesus, Son of the Most High God? I implore You by God that You do not torment me." 8. For He said to him, "Come out of the man, unclean spirit!" 9. Then He asked him, "What is your name?"

And he answered, saying, "My name is Legion; for we are many." Oh 10. Also he begged Him earnestly that He would not send them out of the country. 11. Now a large herd of swine was feeding there near the mountains. 12. So all the demons begged Him, saying, "Send us to the swine, that we may enter them." 13. And at once Jesus gave them permission. Then the unclean spirits went out and entered the swine (there were about two thousand); and the herd ran violently down the steep place into the sea, and drowned in the sea.'

The very presence of Jesus in this case caused the demons that had tormented this man to bow and surrender. There are no evil spirits that have tormented you for years that will not leave in the presence of Jesus. Worship him and let his presence overwhelm you and take charge of your life.

Jesus himself is love. God is love. His presence comes with love that nobody can ever give to you. Have you ever experienced that presence? The moments that the Holy spirit and I have an experience during worship are my best times. So much love, so much peace, something I cannot explain in words. If you have never experienced this, please start having more times of worship and you will never regret.

Jesus is the prince of peace. Isn't it not ironical how much we fail to seek the peace of God rather than peg our peace in our possessions, souses, or even children?

Isaiah 9:6

6 For unto us a Child is born,

Unto us a Son is given;

And the government will be upon His shoulder.

And His name will be called

Wonderful, Counselor, Mighty God,

Everlasting Father, Prince of Peace

I am not refuting that some situations are very story and painful, no; I am simply saying that even in the midst of the storm and pain, you can get your joy, peace and oil of gladness.

Isiah 61: 3 to give them the oil of gladness instead of the spirit of mourning and the garment of praise instead of the spirit of heaviness.

<u>The power of Prayer</u>

The only difference between uncle P, Brian, and I is that I lived to tell my story. The Lord was gracious enough to send someone to pray for me and I am forever grateful for that. You could be in the same situation that I was, and the lord has sent me to you or your loved one through this piece of writing. You can never underestimate the power of prayer. It is paramount to seek a man of God for prayer if you are not in a position to, but the truth is after you have done a sincere praise and worship and thanksgiving, the presence of the lord will be right there and will empower you to pray for yourself. You just need to ask the Holy Spirit to help you worship in truth and pray according to the will of the father.

Suicide is a spirit which the lord has given you power and authority to rebuke and render it powerless in your life and that of your loved one.

Luke 10:19.

Behold, I give you the authority to trample on serpents and scorpions, and over all the power of the enemy, and nothing shall by any means hurt you.

Matthew 18:18.

"Assuredly, I say to you, whatever you bind on earth will be bound in heaven, and whatever you loose on earth will be loosed in heaven. 19. "Again I say to you that if two of you agree on earth concerning anything that they ask, it will be done for them by My Father in heaven. 20. For where two or three are gathered together in My name, I am there in the midst of them."

God has given us authority to bind all demons, all evil spirits, and when we bind them they are also bound in heaven, Hallelujah!

Let's pray;

"Father in the name of Jesus, you've given us power and authority to trample all snakes and scorpions and overcome all the powers of the enemy. We take that power and in the name of Jesus, we come against the spirit of suicide our reader or his or her loved one in the name of Jesus Christ! We bind all forces of death that want to take our reader today or their loved one in the name of Jesus Christ. The word of God says that whatever two agree here on earth shall be established. We then agree that in the name of Jesus our reader and his or her loved ones shall not die but live to see the goodness of the lord in the land of the living. You spirit of suicide, I come against you in the name of Jesus! I arrest you and I bind you in the name of Jesus. I cast you out and send you to the bottomless pit. You will return no more in the name of Jesus! Let's say Amen!"

Our God has had our prayers and that spirit of death and suicide in your life is broken. You only need to believe and when the you feel like you need to end your life, remember you have been given the power of that spirit and all you need is to rebuke and bind the spirit. It is paramount to quote the word of God, the enemy trembles at hearing the word of God as it is a double sword.

If your loved one is suicidal. Rebuke the demonic spirit in the same of Jesus. Sometimes you may be required to fast in regards to the same. If the lord puts it in your heart, laying a sacrifice at the altar is also advised.

Agree with God on what he says about you and your loved one concerning life by claiming and believing in his word.

John 10:10

the enemy came to kill, still, and destroy, but I have come that you may have life and life in abundance.

Psalms 27:13

But I still believe that I will live to see the goodness of God in the land of the living.

Psalms 91:15

With long life I will satisfy him, And show him My salvation."

Proverbs 18:21

Death and life is in the power of the tongue, And those who love it will eat its fruit.

Anna(not her real name) were experiencing carbon monoxide poisoning in their bedroom from a jiko they had placed in the seating room before sleeping. They woke up to realize that they would not move, and something was wrong. Anna started to claim that she would not die but live to see the goodness of God in her life. However, her husband of 26days to be precise was silent all through. Their call for help was unsuccessful as the neighbors thought they were being attacked by thugs so they locked themselves and called the police. But when the police arrived, the husband had passed on. Anna believes her confession and claiming the word of God in her situation preserved her life. Claiming the word of God in your situation whether it's healing, poverty, or life brings life and a turn around.

<h1 style="text-align: center;"><u>The power of Thanksgiving</u></h1>

Psalms 100:4

Enter into His gates with thanksgiving, into His courts with praise. Be thankful to Him, bless His name. 5. For the Lord *is* good; His mercy *is* everlasting, And His truth *endures* to all generations.

Psalms 100 teaches us that the key to the gates of his throne is thanksgiving! In the midst of the storm, there are many things that the lord has done for you without even asking. For example, he has given you life, and has preserved you from death. There are times that you also went to him with a prayer and he answered you. Make a list and you will realize how good God has been to you even in the midst of your pain.

Can you imagine what happens when you access the gates of heaven? There is everything you need.

Psalms 103:1-4

Praise the LORD, my soul; all my inmost being, praise His holy name. Praise the LORD, my soul, and forget not all His benefits — who forgives all your sins and heals all your diseases, who redeems your life from the pit and crowns you with love and compassion.

Colossians 3:15-17

Let the peace of Christ rule in your hearts, since as members of one body you were called to peace. And be thankful. Let the message of Christ dwell among you richly as you teach and admonish one another with all wisdom through psalms, hymns, and songs from the Spirit, singing to God with gratitude in your hearts.

Hebrews 13:15

Through Jesus, therefore, let us continually offer to God a sacrifice of praise — the fruit of lips that openly profess His name

Thanksgiving causes the Lord to answer to you speedily while you are in trouble

Psalms 50:

14. Offer to God thanksgiving, And pay your vows to the Most High. 15.Call upon Me in the day of trouble; I will deliver you, and you shall glorify Me."

Offering a sacrifice of Thanksgiving causes the Lord to answer you in the day of trouble.

The power of forgiveness

After two years of bitterness, the lord asked me to forgive this person who had hurt me deeply. I would go to the Lord during worship time in church and cry a river. You would easily mistake me for a deep worshipper but sadly, instead of taking the moment to reverence the goodness, greatness and love of God in his heavy presence, all I would do was cry over that very person who had hurt me. I still can't believe I wasted so much time being bitter with someone who was never worth it instead of spending my time worshipping the lord. I am however grateful that I took the hurt to the Lord because he eventually bound up my broken heart.

I debated with the lord on the issue of forgiving this person. I felt that he had done a lot of harm to let him go without paying for his crime. I felt forgiving him was doing him an underserved favor. Nevertheless, after a few months of the Lord consistently kept putting the same message in my heart; forgive him. I walked into his house one evening, and told him that I forgive him of all the harm he had caused me. I will never forget the feeling I had while walking out of that house! I felt like a very heavy load had been lifted off my shoulders! I felt free! I felt a sudden peace wash over my soul. I wondered why I had never forgiven him sooner instead of carrying that heavy load all over my shoulders for so many months, while he was carrying on with his life, happy and free.

One person said that unforgiveness is like drinking poison and expecting the other person to die. The person that hurt you is not in pain, he or she is carrying on life happy and free, while you are here drowning yourself in bitterness. He or she is not that important to control your life in that approach.

Come with me; let's see what Jesus says about forgiveness.

Matthew 18: 21-22

"Then Peter came to Jesus and asked, 'Lord, how many times shall I forgive my brother or sister who sins against me? Up to seven times?' Jesus answered, 'I tell you, not seven times, but seventy-seven times.'"

Matthew 6: 14-15

"For if you forgive other people when they sin against you, your heavenly Father will also forgive you. But if you do not forgive others their sins, your Father will not forgive your sins."

Colossians 3:13

"Bear with each other and forgive one another if any of you has a grievance against someone. Forgive as the Lord forgave you."

Ephesians 4: 31-32

"Get rid of all bitterness, rage and anger, brawling and slander, along with every form of malice. Be kind and compassionate to one another, forgiving each other, just as in Christ God forgave you.

Mark 11:25

 "And when you stand praying, if you hold anything against anyone, forgive them, so that your Father in heaven may forgive you your sins."

Matthew 6:9-15

"This, then, is how you should pray: 'Our Father in heaven, Hallowed be your name, Your kingdom come, Your will be done, On earth as it is in heaven. Give us today our daily bread. And forgive us our debts, As we also have forgiven our debtors. And lead us not into temptation, but deliver us from the evil one.'"

Mark 11:25

25 And when you stand praying, if you hold anything against anyone, forgive them, so that your Father in heaven may forgive you your sins."

Can you imagine going to hell because you simply never forgave that person? Probably your spouse cheated on you, and it caused you so much pain. He or she is not worth losing your soul to hell. God forgives you only if you forgive.

Ask the lord to help you forgive the person. The Lord understands our weaknesses and he will be faithful to help you forgive the person. Forgiveness will be the beginning of your freedom and healing.

Forgiveness is simply taking off a very heavy load off your shoulders and putting it on the Lord to carry it for you. God is a vengeful and all you need to do is go to him and ask for his justice to prevail in your case. The Lord Jesus is our advocate in the courts of heaven and he knows your pain, if you allow him to advocate for your case, "wow!" what a great turn of events will you experience.

Romans 12:19

19 Do not take revenge, my dear friends, but leave room for God's wrath, for it is written: "It is mine to avenge; I will repay," says the Lord.

Proverbs 20:22

22 Do not say, "I'll pay you back for this wrong!" Wait for the LORD, and he will avenge you

Psalms 94:1-2

1 The LORD is a God who avenges. O God who avenges, shine forth. 2 Rise up, Judge of the earth; pay back to the proud what they deserve.

Hebrews 4:15

For we do not have a high priest who is unable to empathize with our weaknesses, but we have one who has been tempted in every way, just as we are—yet he did not sin

<u>The power of the Holy Communion</u>

The sacrifice of Jesus Christ on the cross is the covenant that restores us to the father through salvation by the blood of the lamb. It is the covenant that gives us the legal right to be the sons of God and hence inherit the kingdom of God.

Jesus speaking recommended us to take the Holy Communion in rememberance of the cross.

CHAPTER 5

SALVATION

Are you born again? Do you know Jesus Christ as your personal savior? If not; you have a ticket to hell!

John 14:6.

Jesus said to him, "I am the way, the truth, and the life. No one comes to the Father except through me.

You cannot go to the father in heaven unless through Jesus Christ and by having a relationship with him through salvation, there are only two places after death; hell or heaven.

Salvation is accepting a personal relationship with Jesus Christ by allowing the Holy Spirit to dwell in you. You must also confess with your mouth that Jesus is Lord over your life and believe in your heart.

Romans 10:9

If you declare with your mouth, "Jesus is Lord," and believe in your heart that God raised him from the dead, you will be saved.

Acts 4:12

12 Salvation is found in no one else, for there is no other name under heaven given to mankind by which we must be saved.

Suicide is not the only ticket to hell but all unrighteousness. You cannot be righteous by yourself but only by walking with the Holy Spirit who guides you and convicts you to repent while you err.

Salvation has nothing to do with the church you attend! You will not give an account of your deeds together with the church, but alone. The only ticket to heaven is Jesus. Sometimes I have spoken salvation to some people and the first response I got was, "I am catholic', we do not believe in that kind of stuff.' Unfortunately, the only way you can go to the father is through Jesus Christ, not through your catholic church, or Pentecostal church, or whatever religion you are in. Please make the right choice while you still have some time.

Romans 14:12

So then each one of us will give an account of himself to God

Ecclesiastes 12:14
For God will bring every act to judgment, everything which is hidden, whether it is good or evil.

What will you tell your maker on that day? What will he tell you in return? Will you be cast to hell to burn forever simply because you were never willing to accept him?

If you would want to accept Jesus as your personal savior, please say this prayer with me;

Father in the name of Jesus, I come before your presence. I ask for forgiveness of my sins through the blood of Jesus Christ that was shed on the cross for me. I repent of all my sins and I accept you as my personal savior. Write my name in the Book of life. From this day, I am born again. Amen.

Revelation 20:15

Anyone whose name was not found written in the book of life was thrown into the lake of fire.

If you have made this prayer with me, congratulations! This is the best decision you have made in your life and heaven is rejoicing with you. Your name has been written in the book of life and I pray that it will stay that way forever.

Luke 15:10

In the same way, I tell you, there is rejoicing in the presence of the angels of God over one sinner who repents

<u>Living a victorious Life</u>

 If you do not go to church, find a bible believing church and start attending. There is power in communion of the brethren.

Study the bible everyday and learn what God says regarding your situation! The bible has all solutions to our problems. God's word is life and dependable. He watches over his word to keep it. You also discover whom God is and his goodness.

Pray every day. Ask the Lord to give you the Holy spirit who will dwell in you and teach you to pray. He will also you comfort and love in all you do. The Holy Spirit our best companion as he is love, counselor and a friend closer like no other.

John 14:16.

And I will pray the Father, and He will give you another Helper, that He may abide with you forever— 17. The Spirit of truth, whom the world cannot receive, because it neither sees Him nor knows Him; but you know Him, for He dwells within you and will be in you.

John 14:26

But the Advocate, the Holy Spirit, whom the Father will send in my name, will teach you all things and will remind you of everything I have said to you.

1 Corinthians 6:19

Do you not know that your bodies are temples of the Holy Spirit, who is in you, whom you have received from God? You are not your own

There is nothing that can take the place of the Holy Spirit in your life. Allow God the creator, the all mighty, God who is love, our comforter, our peace, our savior, the one who forgives our sins, the one who fights our battles, our provider, and I would go on and on. He is all you need as he will guide you and you will never be alone. *Selah*.